better together*

*This book is best read together, grownup and kid.

a kids book about™

ANXIETY

by **Ross Szabo**
Author of *Behind Happy Faces*

a kids book about™

Library of Congress Cataloging-in-Publication Data is available.

This book represents my personal experience and thus is not intended to be representative of every form or example of anxiety as it applies to the many who have experienced it in their lives.

A Kids Book About Anxiety is exclusively available online on the a kids book about website.

To share your stories, ask questions, or inquire about bulk purchases (schools, libraries, and nonprofits), please use the following email address:

hello@akidsbookabout.com

www.akidsbookabout.com

ISBN: 978-1-951253-14-1

Printed in the USA

Interested in inviting Ross Szabo to speak at your school?

Visit: TopYouthSpeakers.com

To my students at Geffen Academy,
I'm forever inspired by your strength

Intro

Kids learn about their physical health from a really young age. They learn about their body, how much water they should drink, what they should eat and who to go to when they feel sick. We don't teach them the same kind of skills with their mental health. We often wait until they are much older or until something is clearly wrong to start a conversation about how to take care of their emotions.

When most people hear the words mental health they tend to think of a person who has a problem. However, mental health isn't having a problem. The actual definition of mental health is how you address challenges in your life. Mental health is communication, healthy relationships, strong coping skills, and how you take care of your mind.

This book is designed to help kids start thinking about their mental health, the same way they think about physical health. It's intended to start conversations to normalize mental health from a young age.

Have you ever felt so nervous that you didn't know what to do?

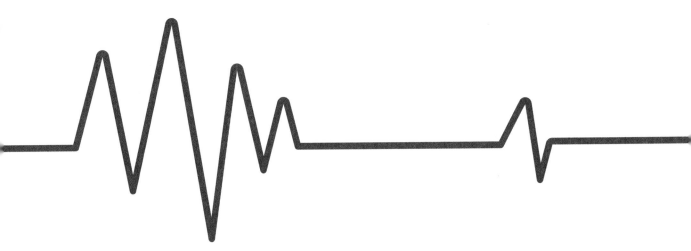

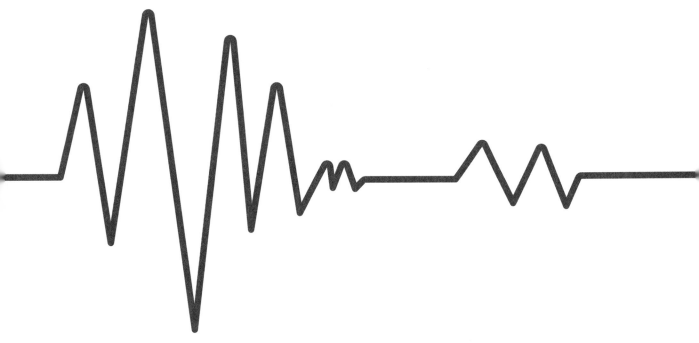

Do you ever feel like you can't calm down no matter how hard you try?

This is a book about the difference between feeling nervous sometimes...

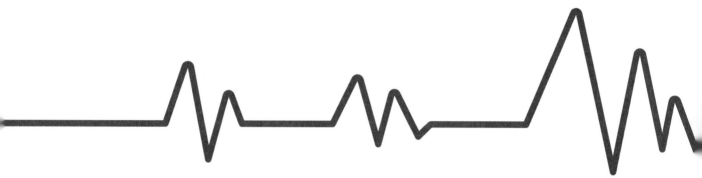

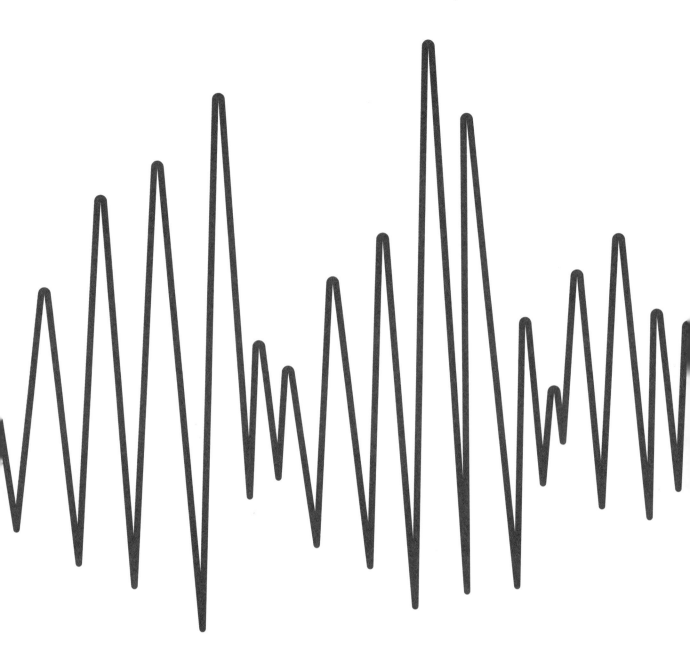

And having anxiety.

This is something I know a lot about, because I've felt anxiety many times in my life.

The story I'm going to tell is about how hard it is to feel anxiety and...

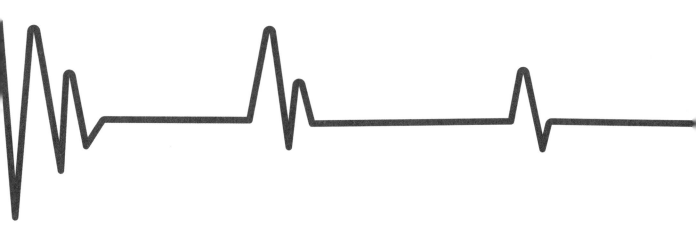

how to build some skills if you or anyone you know ever feels this way.

My name is Ross.

I love recess, chocolate chip cookies, building blanket forts in my room...

throwing a football with my older brother, and I am always wearing my favorite Incredible Hulk t-shirt.

I really like my friends and going to school.

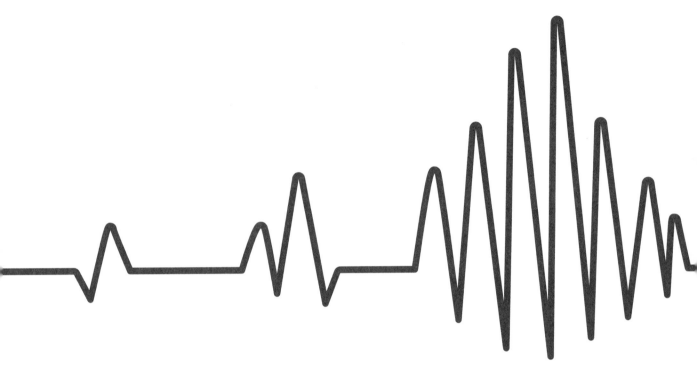

But...

**Sometimes when I'm
sitting in class,**

I start to feel...

Strange.

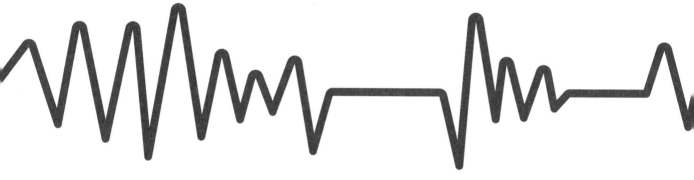

At first, I start to feel like there's a tiny bouncy ball moving from my stomach to my chest.

And as it moves up, it keeps getting bigger.

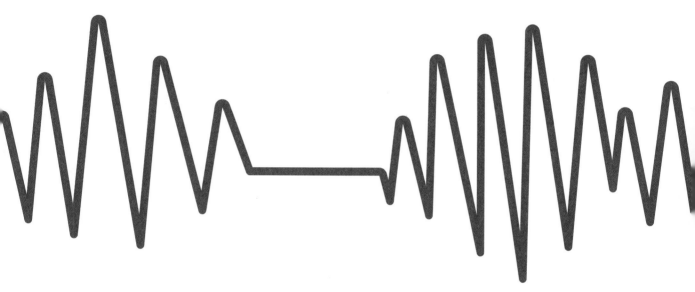

Now it's not the size of a bouncy ball, but a baseball.

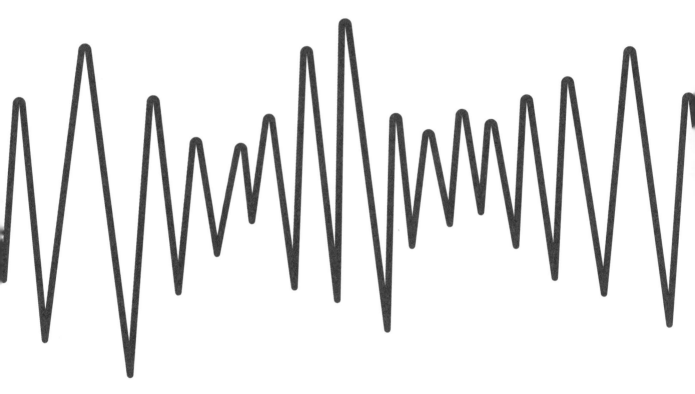

I feel like my heart is beating super fast...

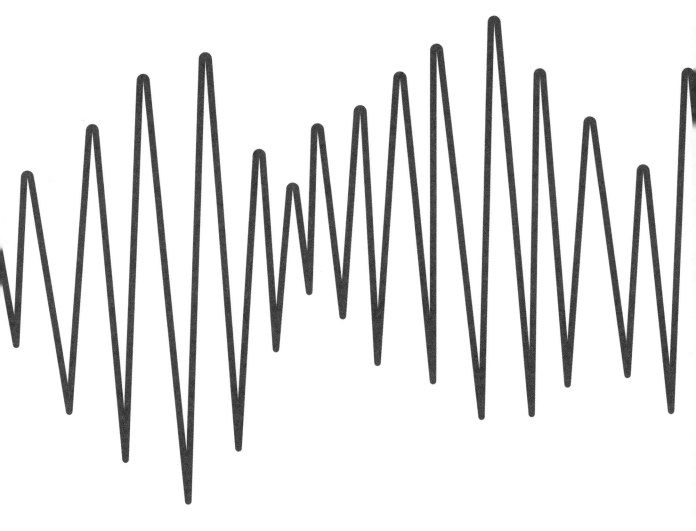

Too fast.

I feel like I need to...

ESC

APE

but I can't.

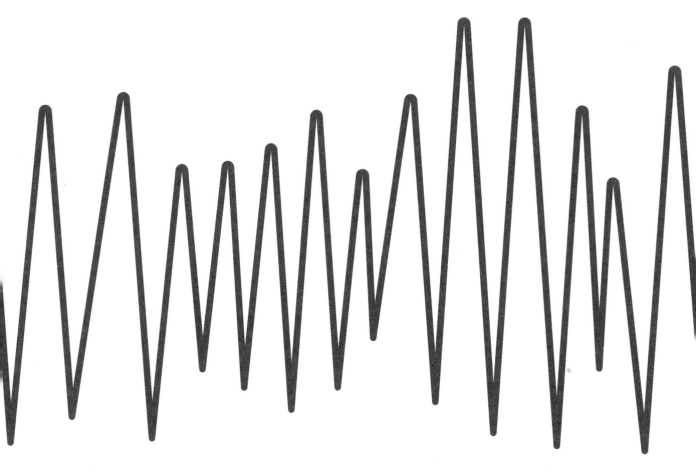

I look around. It seems that
no one else is feeling this way.

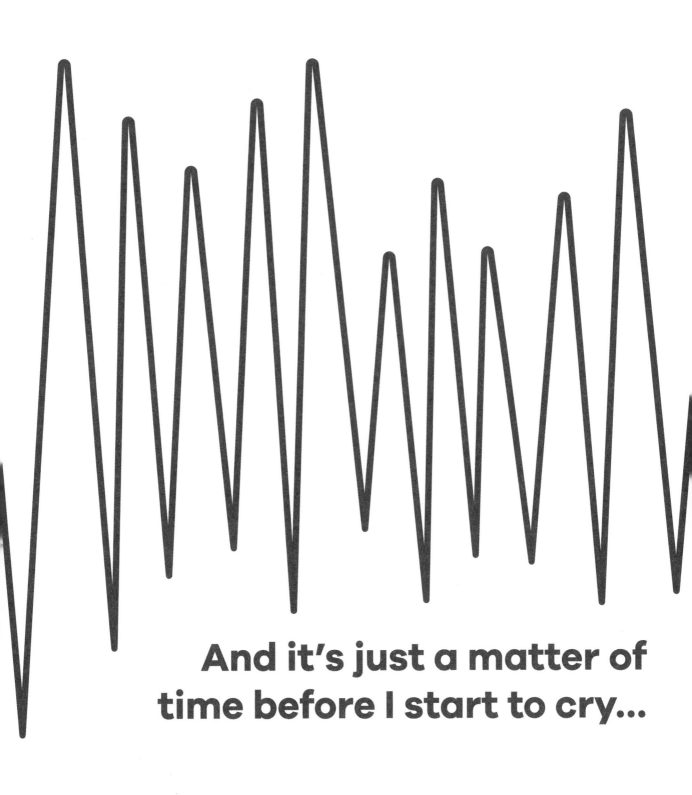

And it's just a matter of
time before I start to cry...

**Now the classroom stops,
and everyone is looking at me.**

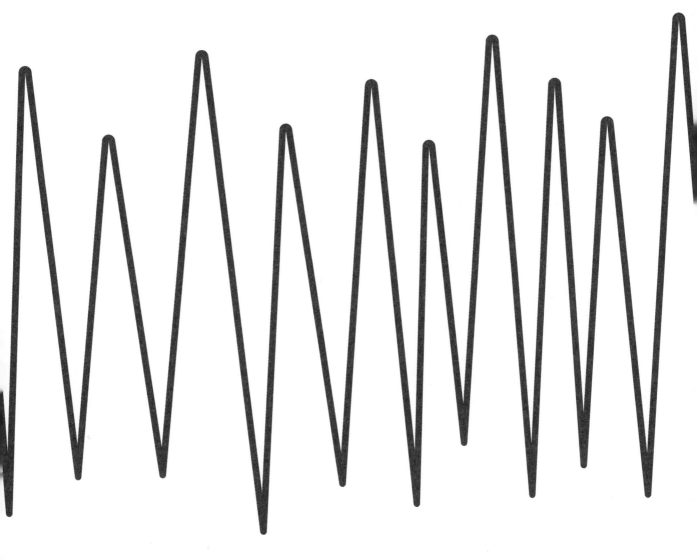

I just want this to stop, but I don't know what to do.

I'm not just having a bad day.

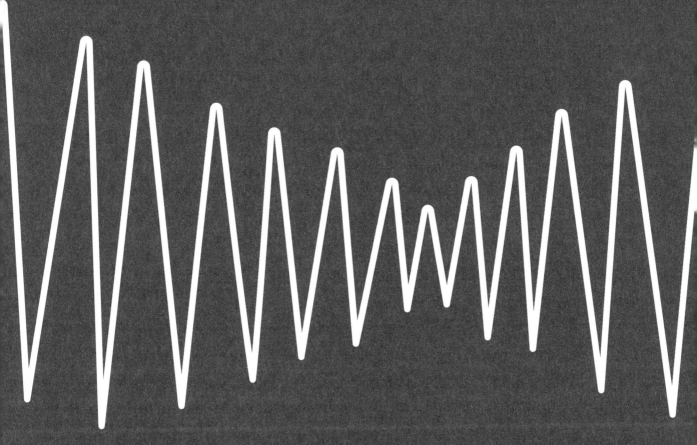

I'm not upset about forgetting my homework.

No one was mean to me.

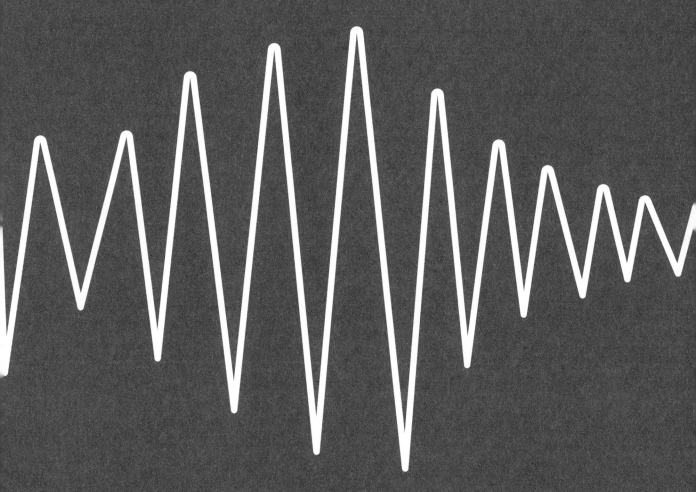

I'm not just nervous...

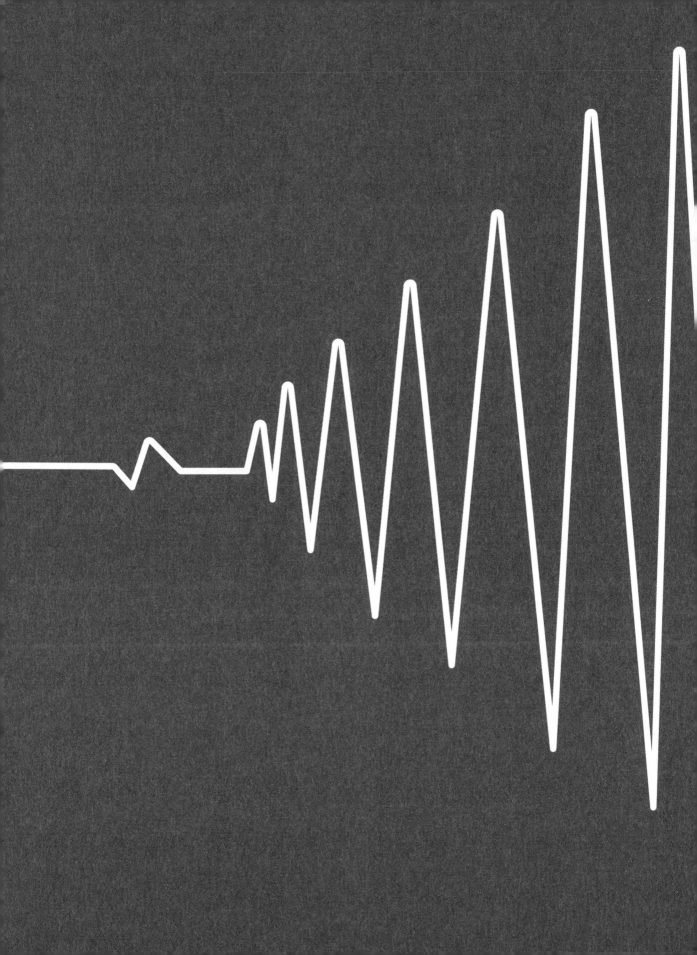

I have anxiety.

Anxiety is an uncontrollable feeling that stops you from doing what you normally do.

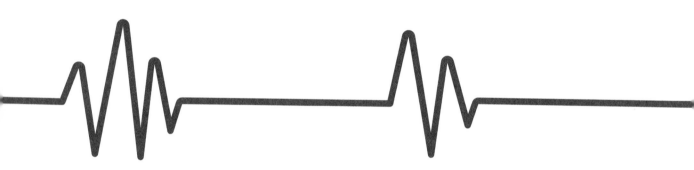

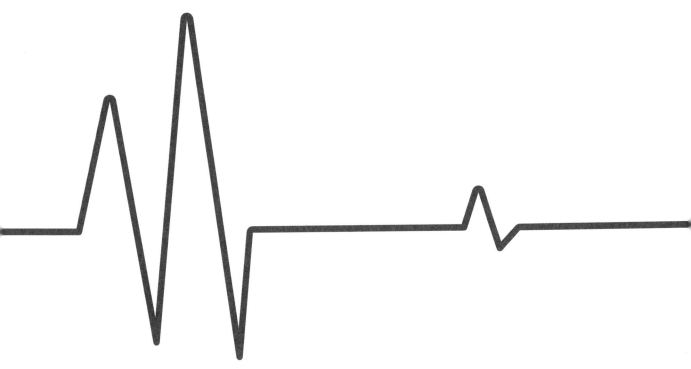

Anxiety is different than just being nervous.

When you're nervous...

it doesn't last that long.

Like before a test, or a game, or before you go to the doctor.

Being nervous is a natural feeling everyone has, it lasts a short time, and goes away.

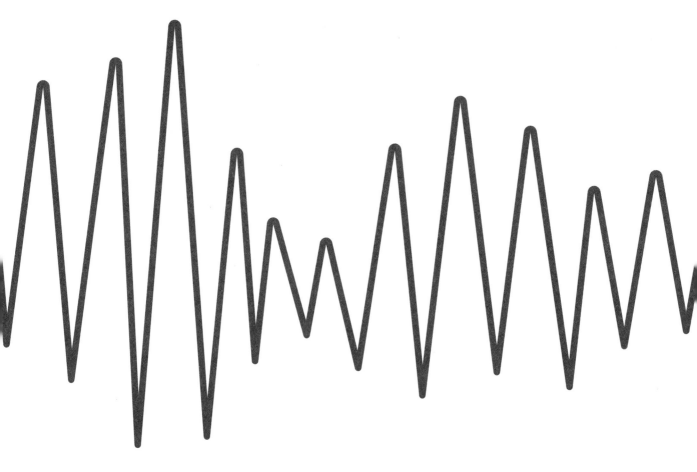

But, anxiety is a feeling that continues to grow over time.

It makes you feel...

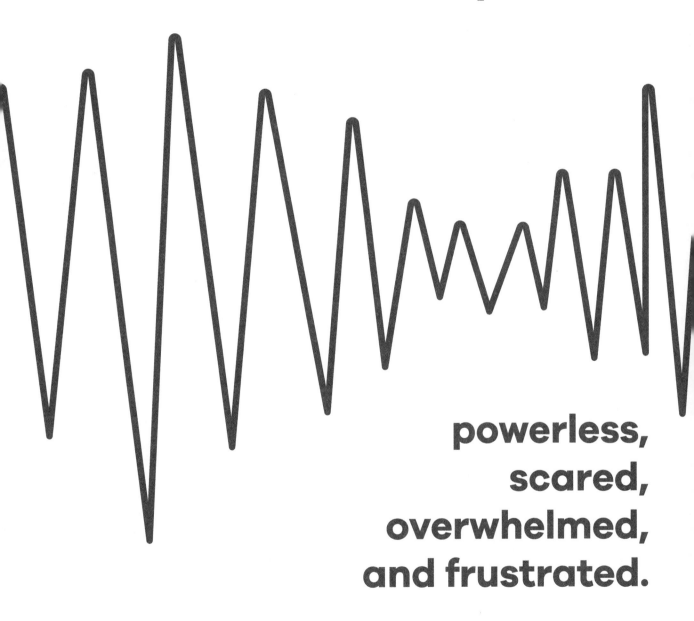

powerless,
scared,
overwhelmed,
and frustrated.

Anxiety makes kids' lives really hard.

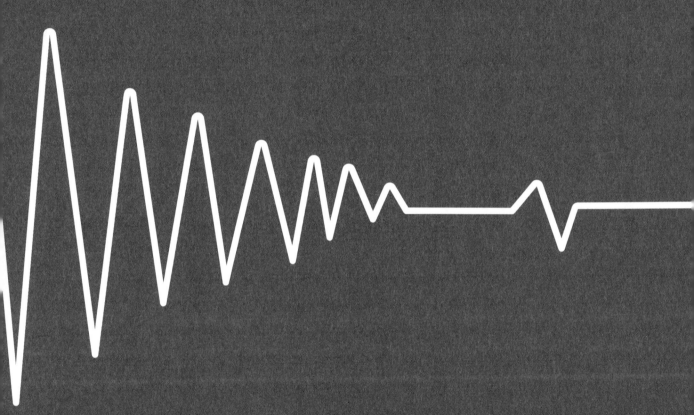

Anxiety doesn't just go away on its own.

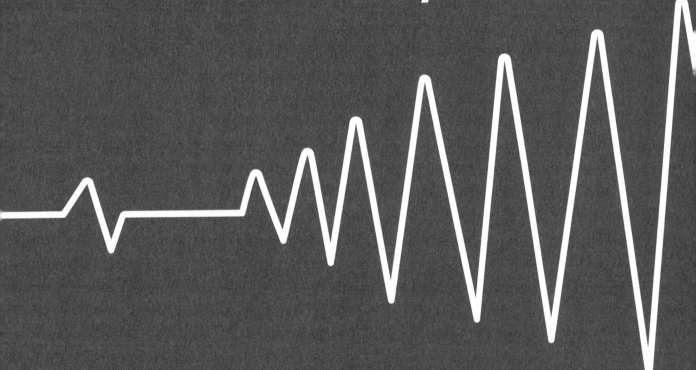

So let me tell my story again...

But this time a little different.

I still like cookies, forts, football, and The Hulk...

And I also like my friends and going to school.

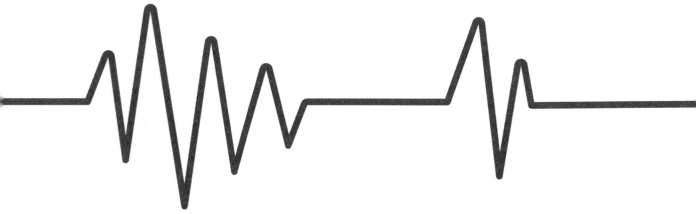

**And sometimes when
I'm in class...**

I start to feel like there's a tiny bouncy ball moving from my stomach to my chest.

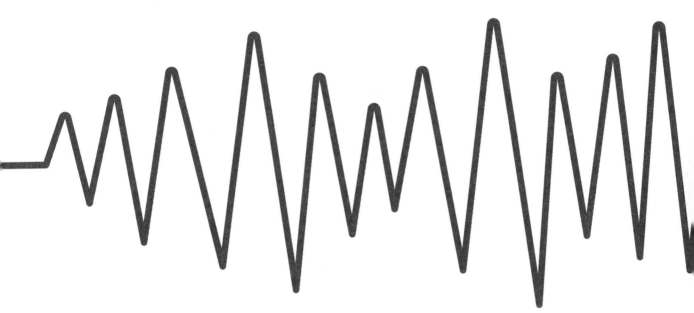

And as it moves up, it keeps getting bigger.

I start to take some deep breaths to keep the bouncy ball from growing.

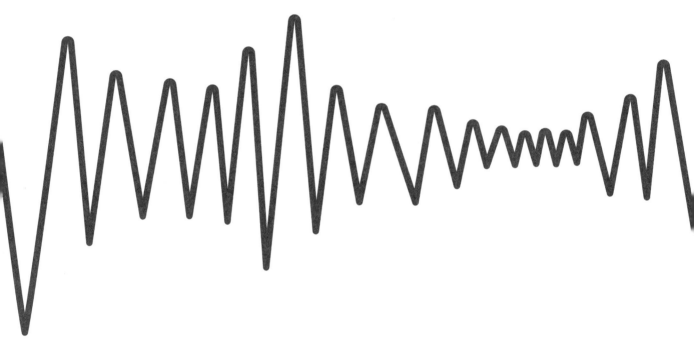

The breaths help slow it down, but now my heart is beating super fast.

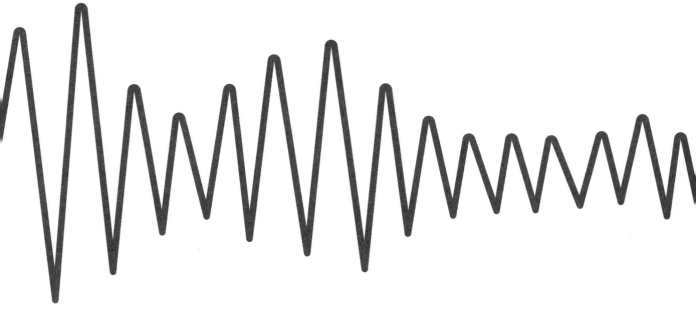

I close my eyes and try to focus
on feeling my breath run
through my chest.

Now I feel warm, like I'm starting to sweat.

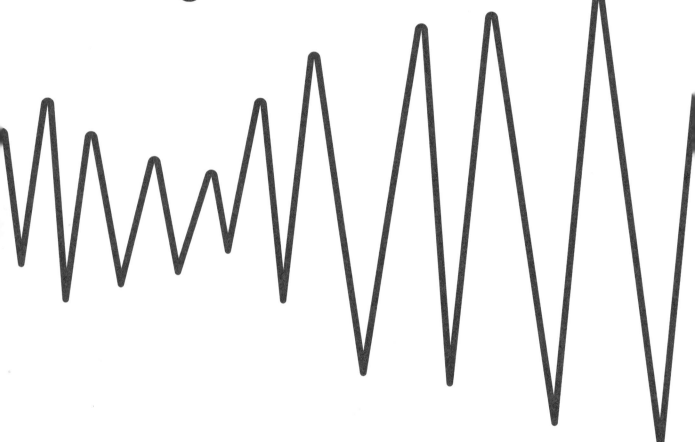

I focus on one spot on my desk.

I stare at the spot and try to block out everything else that is happening.

I feel like my heart isn't racing as fast and my body isn't as warm.

But I'm not sure I can stop
my anxiety.

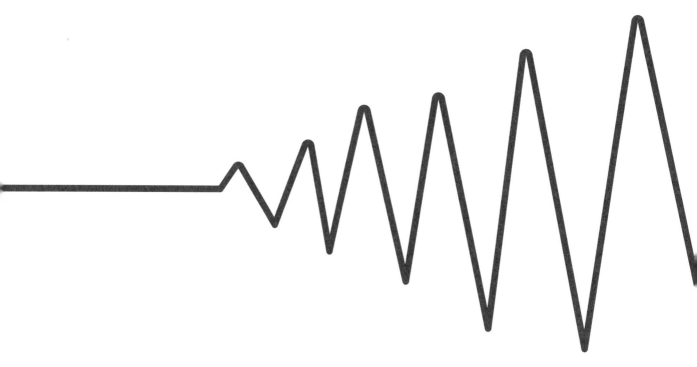

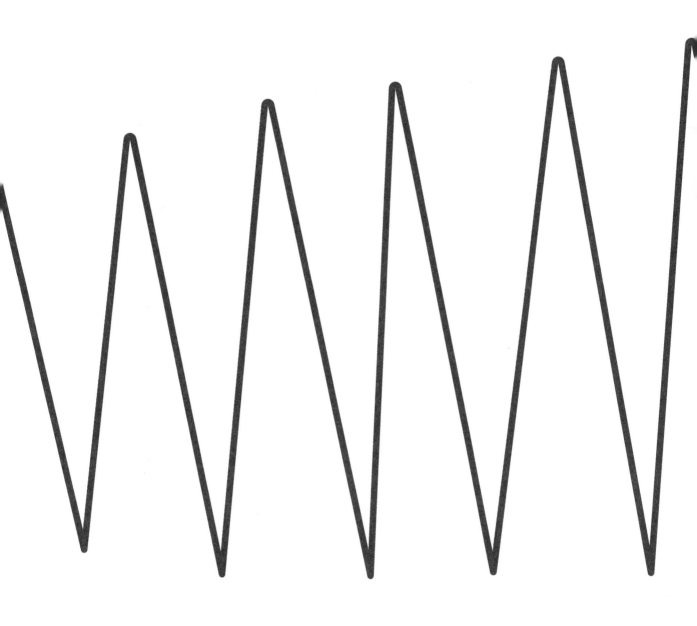

I raise my hand and ask to go to the bathroom.

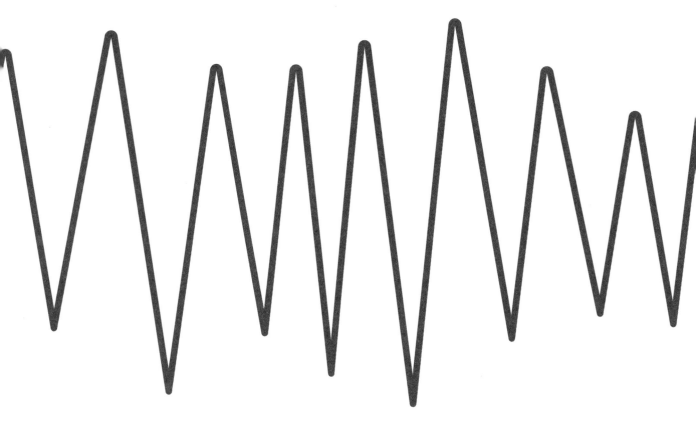

When I get outside of the room,

I start to cry a little bit, but not as much as other times.

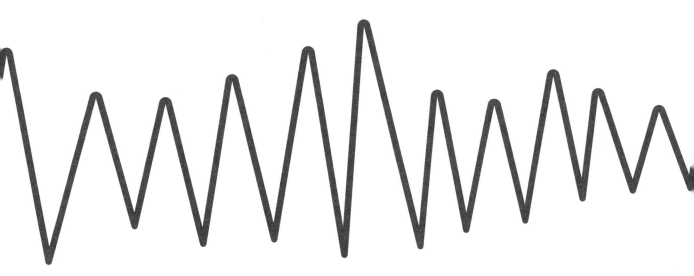

I walk to the bathroom and continue to take deep breaths.

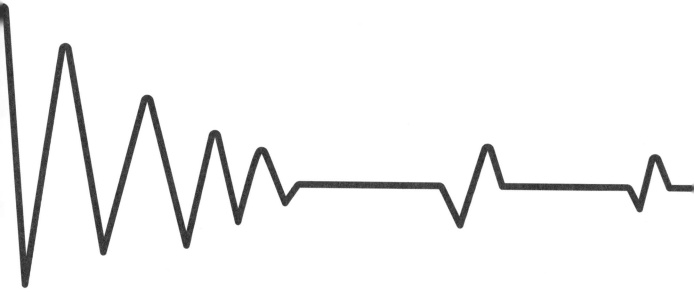

Eventually, I return to class.

After school I tell my parents I had to leave a class because I couldn't stop my anxiety.

My parents told me they support me doing what I need to take care of myself.

Can you tell the difference between the two stories?

**In the first one,
I didn't know what to do,
and my anxiety
takes over.**

**But in the second one, I have
some skills to help with anxiety.**

I learned them from a counselor.

It's someone I talk to about my anxiety who helps me learn how to make sure it doesn't get out of control.

I'm learning to talk to people I trust about anxiety.

I have anxiety...

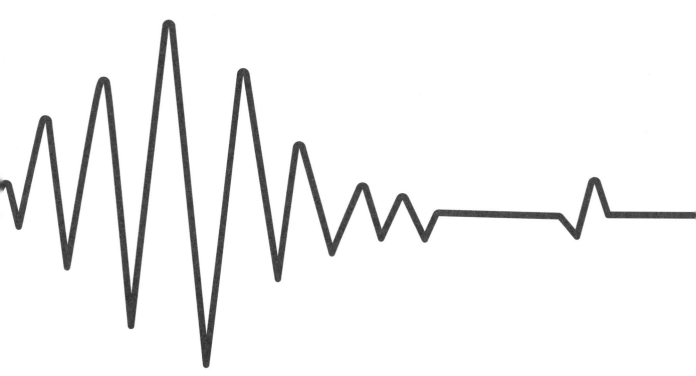

At my friend's house.

Playing basketball.

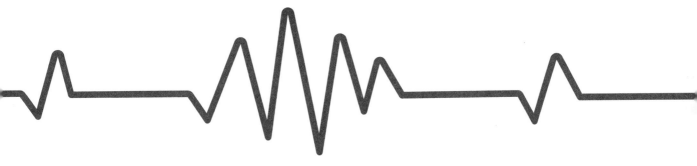

Eating dinner with my family.

Alone in my room.

Luckily, I have support from my friends, my coaches, my parents, and my brothers to help me learn what to do.

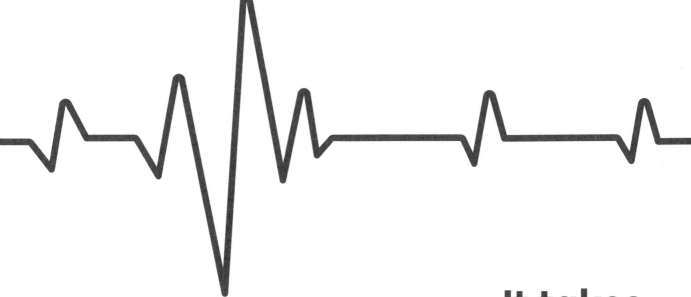

**It takes
a lot of practice
for me to learn what
to do to lessen my anxiety.**

I try to get better each time and I make small steps.

I'm not able to completely stop my anxiety.

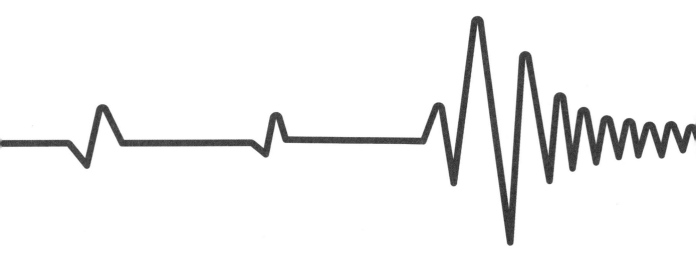

I'm learning how to identify
when it happens and what
to do to slow it down.

From one kid who knows what it's like to have anxiety to anyone reading this book:

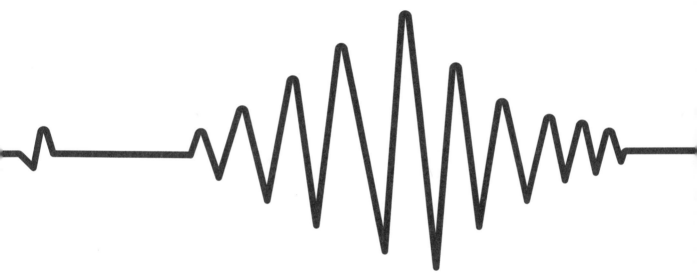

I hope you know
it's ok to not be ok.

Outro

Now that you've read about my story with anxiety, it's your turn to share your own story!

It's helpful for families to talk about any members of their family who have experienced anxiety or other mental health issues. Anxiety is strongly tied to genetics and can skip generations, so make sure to think about grandparents, aunts, uncles, cousins, and everyone in a family.

You can talk about what makes you nervous and how you deal with it. You can talk about times someone has anxiety and how they manage it. The more we talk about it, the easier it may be for someone to share their experience. The beauty of telling our stories is that they can help families heal. Our stories can take us to places we never imagined we would go.

find
more
kids
books
about

belonging, feminism, creativity
money, depression, failure,
gratitude, adventure,
cancer, body image,
and racism.

share
your read*

*Tell somebody, post a photo, or give this book away to share what you care about.

@akidsbookabout